SandCastle™

Baby Mammals

It's a Baby

Opossum!

Kelly Doudna

Consulting Editor, Diane Craig, M.A./Reading Specialist

Published by ABDO Publishing Company, 8000 West 78th Street, Edina, Minnesota 55439.

Printed in the United States.

Editor: Pam Price
Content Developer: Nancy Tuminelly
Cover and Interior Design and Production: Mighty Media
Photo Credits: Digital Vision, Peter Arnold Inc. (John Cancalosi, S.J. Krasemann), ShutterStock

Library of Congress Cataloging-in-Publication Data

Doudna, Kelly, 1963-
  It's a baby opossum! / Kelly Doudna.
    p. cm. -- (Baby mammals)
  ISBN 978-1-60453-028-5
  1. Opossums--Infancy--Juvenile literature. I. Title.

  QL737.M34D68 2008
  599.2'76139--dc22

                       2007036931

SandCastle™ Level: Fluent

SandCastle™ books are created by a team of professional educators, reading specialists, and content developers around five essential components—phonemic awareness, phonics, vocabulary, text comprehension, and fluency—to assist young readers as they develop reading skills and strategies and increase their general knowledge. All books are written, reviewed, and leveled for guided reading, early reading intervention, and Accelerated Reader® programs for use in shared, guided, and independent reading and writing activities to support a balanced approach to literacy instruction. The SandCastle™ series has four levels that correspond to early literacy development. The levels are provided to help teachers and parents select appropriate books for young readers.

| **Emerging Readers** | **Beginning Readers** | **Transitional Readers** | **Fluent Readers** |
| (no flags) | (1 flag) | (2 flags) | (3 flags) |

SandCastle™ would like to hear from you. Please send us your comments and suggestions.
sandcastle@abdopublishing.com

Vital Statistics

for the Opossum

BABY NAME
there is no special name

NUMBER IN LITTER
5 to 20, average 8

WEIGHT AT BIRTH
$\frac{1}{15}$ ounce

AGE OF INDEPENDENCE
4 to 5 months

ADULT WEIGHT
9 to 13 pounds

LIFE EXPECTANCY
1 to 2 years

Opossums are marsupials.
Marsupials are mammals
that have pouches.
The opossum is North
America's only marsupial.

Koalas and kangaroos
are also marsupials.

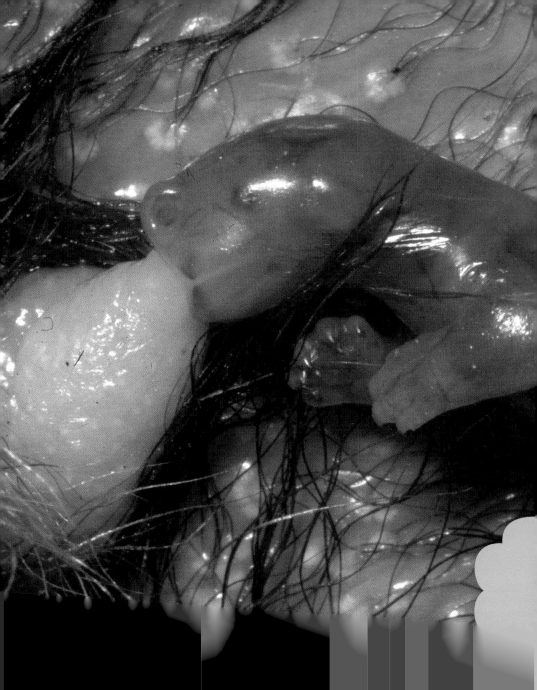

Newborn opossums are not fully developed. They must find their way to the pouch. They continue to grow in the pouch.

A mother opossum can nurse up to 13 babies.

When baby opossums are four or five months old, they are too big to fit in their mother's pouch. Then they ride on her back.

Opossums have prehensile tails. Prehensile tails can be used to grip things and to carry things.

Babies hang by their tails sometimes. Adults are too heavy to do this.

13

Opossums are omnivores. Opossums prefer snails and other insects. They will even eat pet food that has been left outside.

Opossums bluff their way out of dangerous situations. They hiss and open their mouths to show their teeth.

Opossums are famous for playing dead. This confuses predators.

Most opossums do not live longer than two years. The majority are killed by cars. Some are killed by predators, such as owls.

Young opossums do not stay with their mothers for long. They are independent by the time they are five months old.

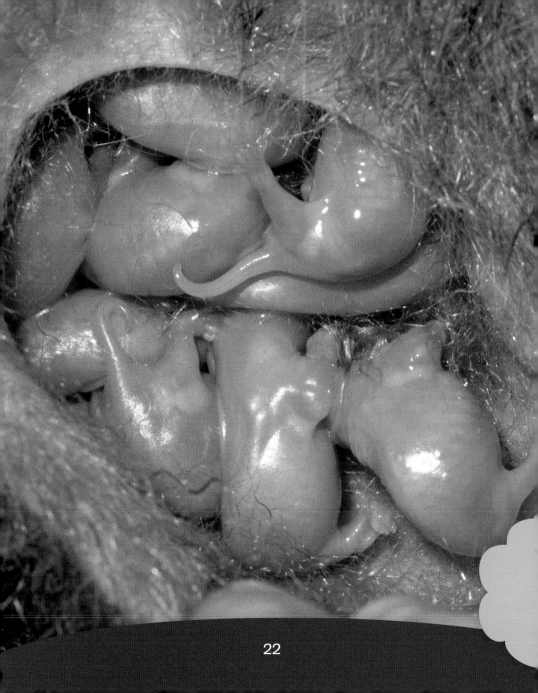

Fun Fact
About the Opossum

A newborn opossum is about as big as a honeybee. Ten newborn opossums could fit in a teaspoon.

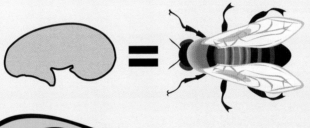

Glossary

bluff – to pretend to be stronger than you really are.

expectancy – an expected or likely amount.

independence – the state of no longer needing others to care for or support you.

majority – a number that is more than half of a total.

marsupial – a mammal in which the female has a pouch in which the young develop.

omnivore – one who eats both meat and plants.

pouch – a pocketlike space on the belly in which marsupials carry their young.

predator – an animal that hunts others.

prehensile – able to wrap around and grasp something.

To see a complete list of SandCastle™ books and other nonfiction titles from ABDO Publishing Company, visit **www.abdopublishing.com**.

8000 West 78th Street, Edina, MN 55439

800-800-1312 • 952-831-1632 fax